Okie Dokie...

So you might need a little help getting started. That's why we've added numbered steps on the left-hand pages.

● Every spread includes a set of step-by-step instructions for drawing something wonderful (or wacky or scary or fun)!

● It's your choice: You can draw from the sample provided, or just do your own thing.

● When you're done drawing, use markers, pens, or colored pencils to complete your masterpiece.

the Eyes Have It!

Always start your drawings from the eyes. Notice the shapes you're drawing and their distance from the eyes.

Here are some good general guidelines to use:
1 Start drawing the nose at one eyeball and end it at the other.
2 Ears look good if they're about level with the middle of the eyeball.
3 The nose is about two eyeballs long.

Let's Get Into Shape!

Your drawing should start with basic shapes: If you can draw these, you can draw just about anything.

Round Shapes

Circle

Oval

Bean

Curved Shapes

Crescent

Guitar

Teardrop

Angular Shapes

Triangle

Square

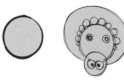

Express Yourself!

Want to know a trick? Adding eyelashes will change a boy into a girl!

Draw different lines around the eyes to give your dinosaur expressions.

Stunned　　　Angry　　　Tired or Sick　　　Worried　　　Crazy

Line It Up!

All of those little drawing marks, lines, and details you see around illustrations help communicate movement and feelings. Check out all of the ones we came up with!

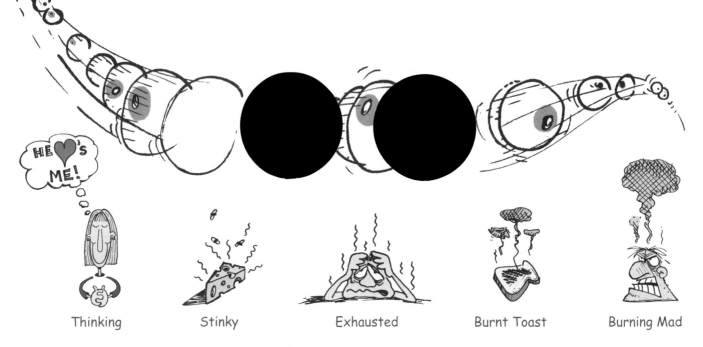

Thinking   Stinky   Exhausted   Burnt Toast   Burning Mad

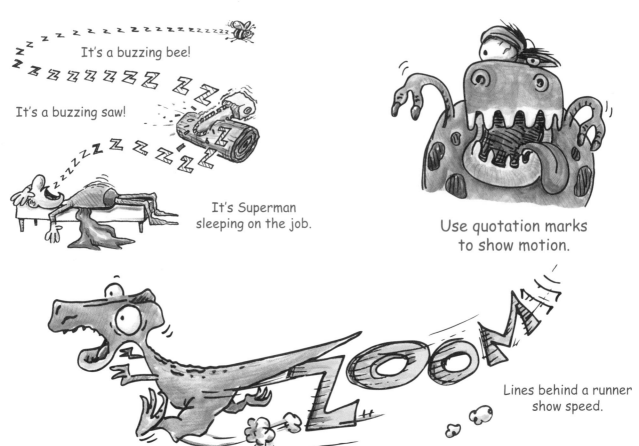

It's a buzzing bee!

It's a buzzing saw!

It's Superman sleeping on the job.

Use quotation marks to show motion.

Lines behind a runner show speed.

practice page

Try drawing your own dinosaur right here on this page.

1. Start with the head. Remember to note where the lines start and end around the eyes.

2. Add a nose, body, and head crest.

3. Next, add a big mouth and the legs.

4. Draw the tail and some eyebrows.

5. Add some shading and . . .

Congratulations! A dinosaur is born!

Shading and Shadows

Your drawings will have more depth and dimension if you add shading and shadows.

Basic Shape	Shade	Shadow

Did you know?

Not every big and extinct animal is a dinosaur. The name dinosaur is used only for those that had a certain type of hip bone. So the long-necked plesiosaur, the porpoise-like ichthyosaur, the lizard-like mosasaur, and the flying pterosaur really weren't dinosaurs, even though they lived in the age of the dinosaurs.

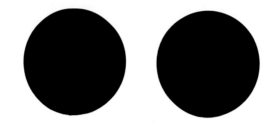

Mosasaurus

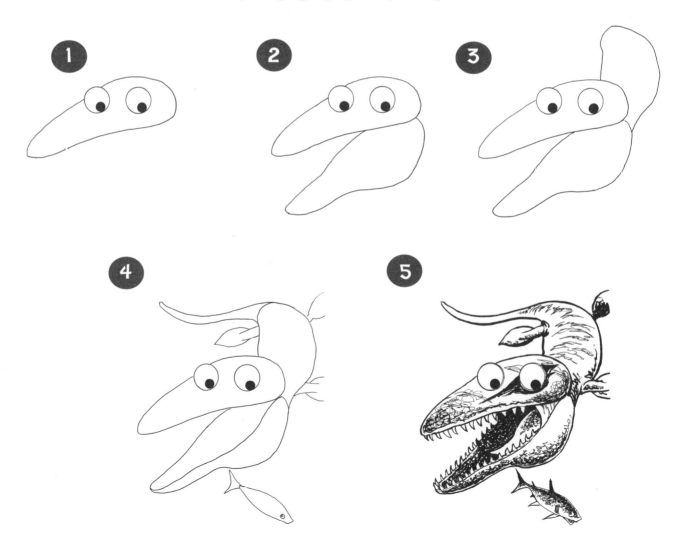

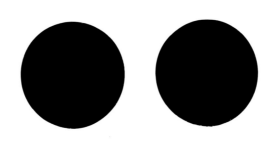

Did you know?

Recently, a 5 foot, 4 inch (162 cm) carnivore skull was found in North Africa. This dinosaur, *Carcharodontosaurus*, was about the size of *Tyrannosaurus rex*. Its teeth were fiercely sharp and looked similar to those of a great white shark.

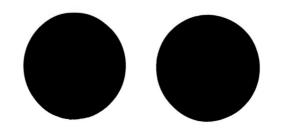

scelidosaurus

Carcharodontosaurus   Confuciusornis

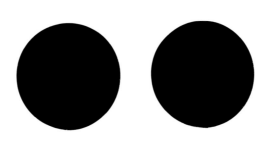

Did you know?

Think you know the names of all the dinosaurs? Think again! There are more than 500 officially named dinosaur species. On average, a new dinosaur species is discovered every six weeks.

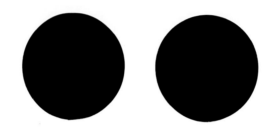

tanystropheus

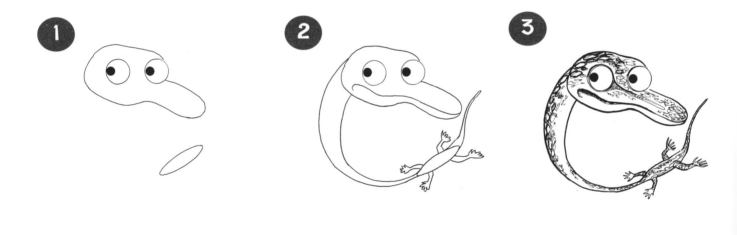

Masiakasaurus

Hovasaurus

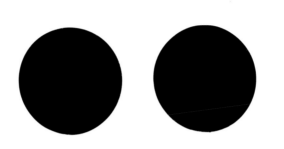

Did you know?

Iguanodons were the second dinosaur species ever classified (early 1800s). An amazing find was made in 1878 when 24 nearly complete skeletons were uncovered in a coal mine more than 1,000 feet (305 m) underground.

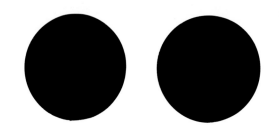

Iguanodon

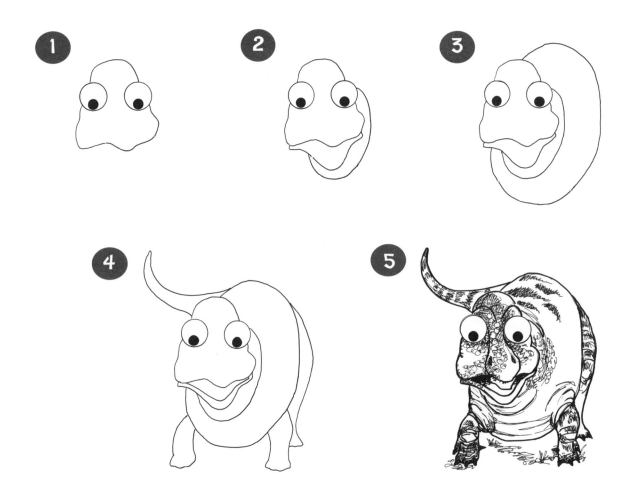

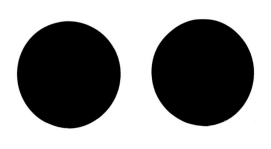

Did you know?

Pterosaurs (also known as pterodactyls) ruled the skies of the Mesozoic. Unlike birds, however, they had no feathers. Some had a fine fur-like covering on their skin—insulation that indicates they were warm-blooded.

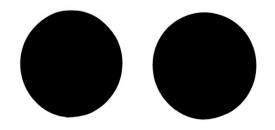

Lesothosaurus

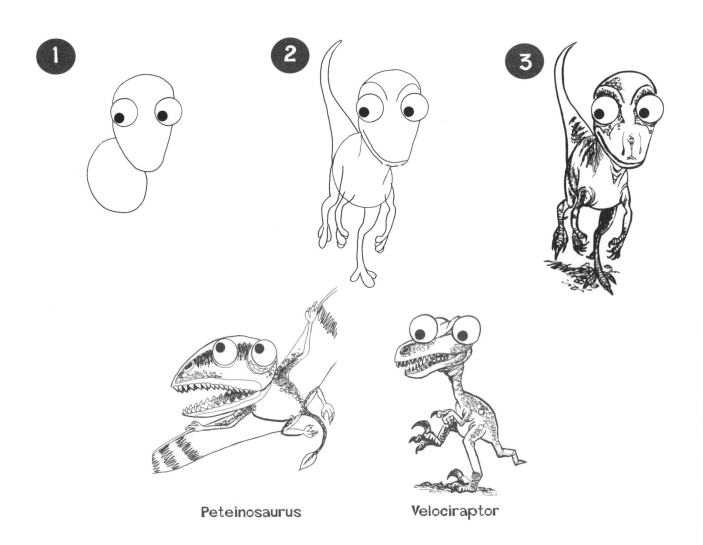

Peteinosaurus   Velociraptor

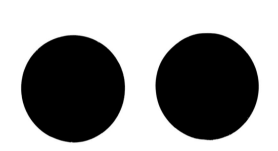

Did you know?

Torosaurus was a huge ceratopsid. At 15,000 pounds (6,800 kg), it could hold its own against *Tyrannosaurus rex*. *Torosaurus* also has the record of having the largest skull of any land animal ever—almost 9 feet (3 m) long!

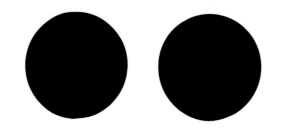

Styracosaurus

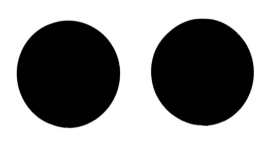

Did you know?

Some scientists believe that the bony plates of the *Stegosaurus* and the spiny sails of the *Spinosaurus* helped to heat or cool the animals. Other scientists believe that these showy parts made the animals more attractive to potential mates.

Psephoderma

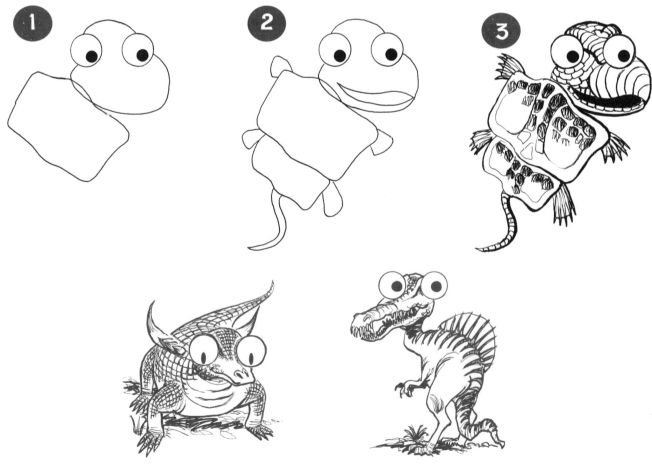

Desmatosuchus   Spinosaurus

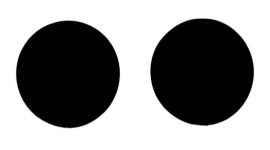

Did you know?

The skeleton of *Apatosaurus* was given the wrong skull for more than 100 years. Not until 1979 did scientists discover the mistake, even though the correct skull had been dug up almost 70 years earlier.

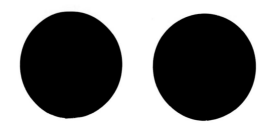

Leptoceratops

Apatosaurus   Climatius

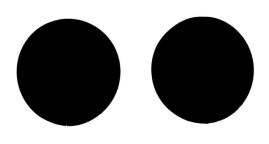

Did you know?

Injuries on dinosaur bones can show us who ate whom. *Tyrannosaurus* teeth fit perfectly in holes found in some *Triceratops* bones, and *Allosaurus* teeth fit into some marks on *Stegosaurus* bones. One healed bite mark on the tail of an *Edmontosaurus* skeleton shows that it was attacked by a *Tyrannosaurus* but got away.

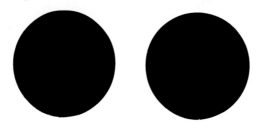

Megalosaurus

Triceratops

Kentrosaurus

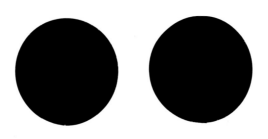

Did you know?

The first *Triceratops* bones found were once thought to belong to a giant extinct *Bison*. Later, more complete skulls were found, which showed the mistake.

Westlothiana

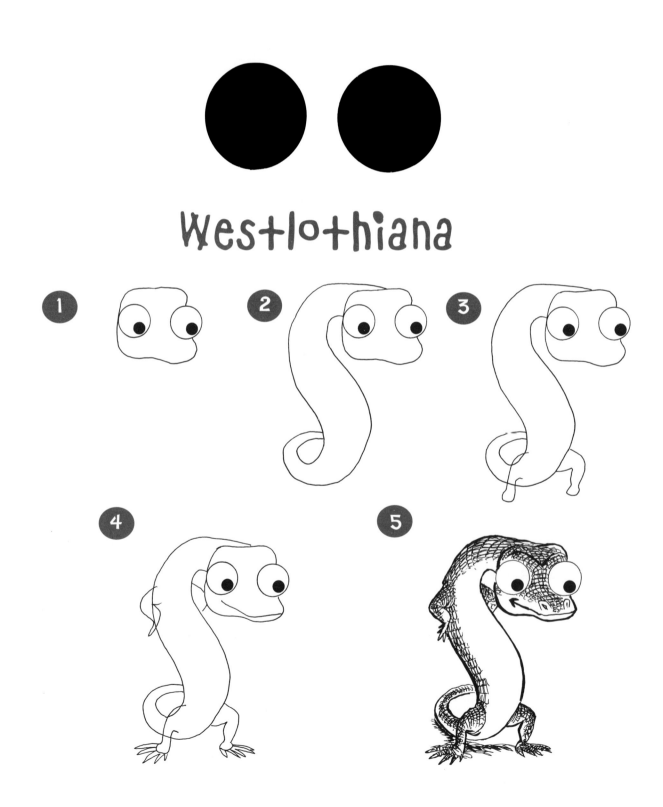

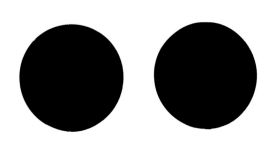

Did you know?

Stegosaurus is said to have had a brain the size of a walnut.
In reality, it was more the size and shape of a bent hot dog.
Sauropods' brains were even smaller compared
to their huge bodies.

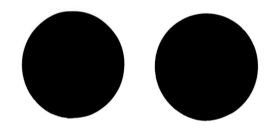

stegosaurus

Camarasaurus   Allosaurus

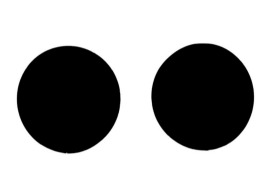

Did you know?

Ankylosaurs were the armored tanks of the dinosaur world.
They had wide, low bodies covered with bony plates in their skin.
Taking a bite out of an ankylosaur would likely
mean a broken tooth for predators.

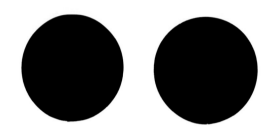

Hypacrosaurus

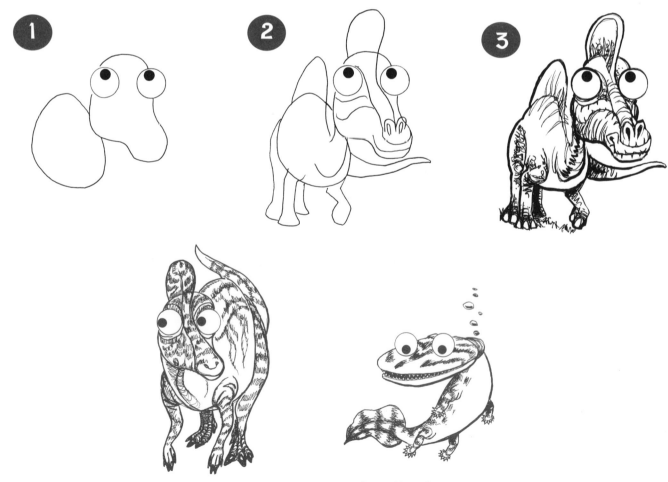

Corythosaurus   Acanthostega

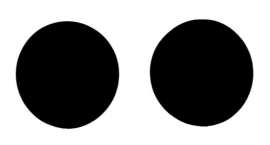

Did you know?

Were dinosaurs warm-blooded or cold-blooded?
Yes! Dinosaurs evolved from cold-blooded reptiles, but their descendants were the warm-blooded birds. Fossil evidence shows that certain dinosaurs had traits of both warm- and cold-blooded animals.

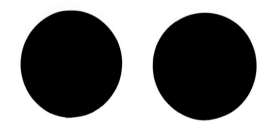

Tapejara

Beipiaosaurus   Stegoceras

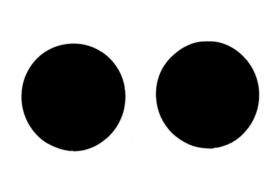

Did you know?

The largest two-legged animal—and also the largest carnivore—to ever live on Earth might be the *Giganotosaurus* ("giant southern lizard"). It was about 46 feet (14 m) long, 12 feet (4 m) tall, and weighed more than 8 tons (7 metric tons). Its skull alone was 6 feet (2 m) long!

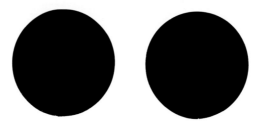

Diadectes

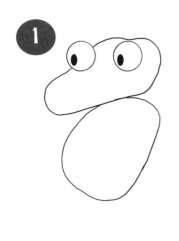

Giganotosaurus

Oviraptor

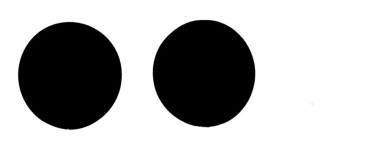

Did you know?

Today, many types of birds return year after year to the same place to lay their eggs. Apparently, so did some dinosaurs. In Spain, one site contained 90,000 eggs laid over a period of 10,000 years.

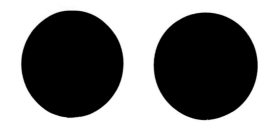

Barosaurus

Scutosaurus   Caudipteryx

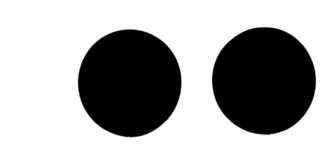

Did you know?

Dinosaurs were probably not very smart. Compared to their body size, their brains were small. The smartest, *Troodon*, was probably only as smart as an ostrich.

troodon

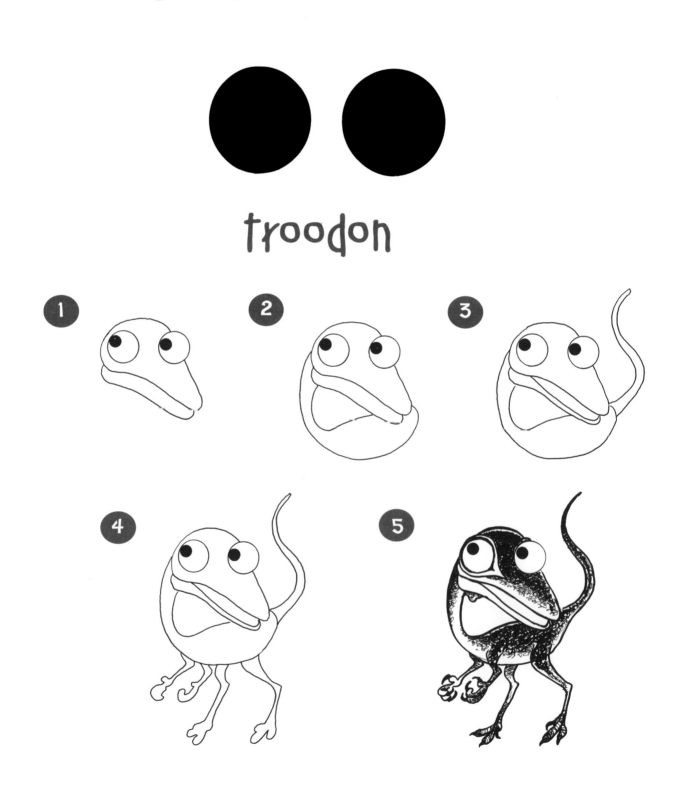

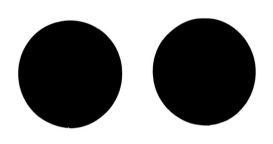

Did you know?

Most reptiles lay eggs. Ichthyosaurs, however, had live births. How do we know? An *Ichthyosaurus* has been found fossilized as it was giving birth, just as the baby was exiting the mother. Truly a one-in-a-million fossil.

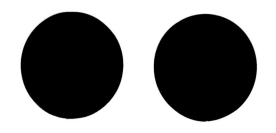

Ichthyosaurus

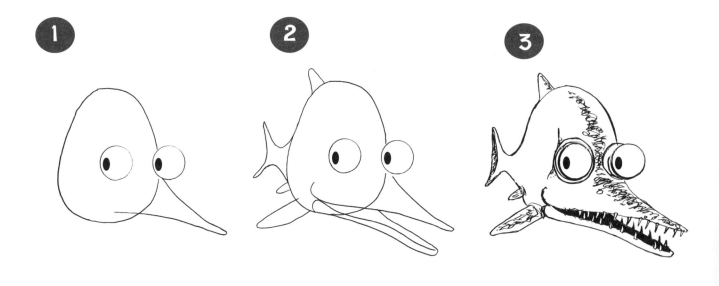

Henodus

Nothosaurus

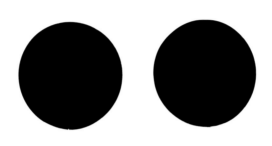

Did you know?

Even though dragons are mythical creatures, they were likely based on dinosaur fossils. In fact, the countries we associate most often with dragons, China and England, both have important dinosaur fossils. The best example is the dragon-looking dinosaur *Dracorex hogwartsia*.

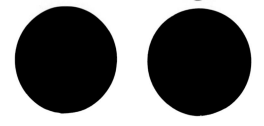

tarbosaurus

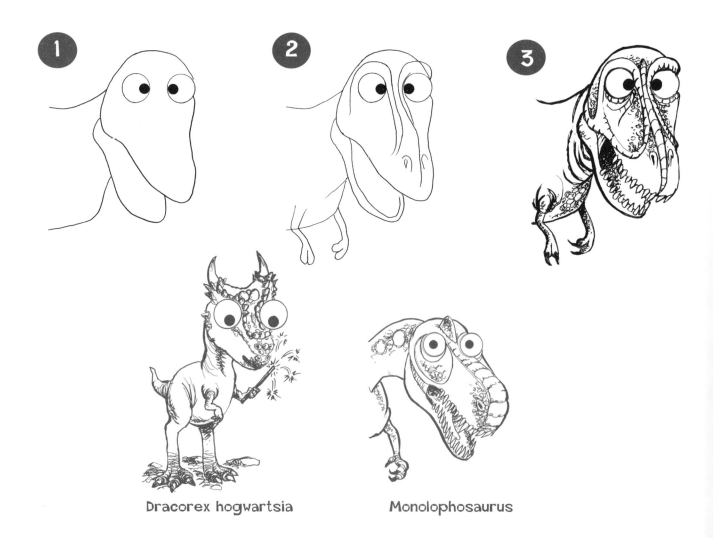

Dracorex hogwartsia   Monolophosaurus

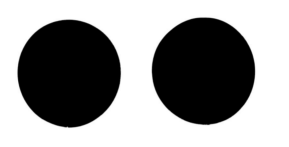

Did you know?

There are two dinosaurs with female names: *Maiasaura* (which means "good mother lizard") and *Leaellynasaura*, named for a little girl, Leaellyn Rich, who asked her parents to find a dinosaur fossil for her. Since her parents are paleontologists, they did!

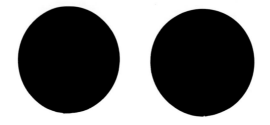

Maiasaura

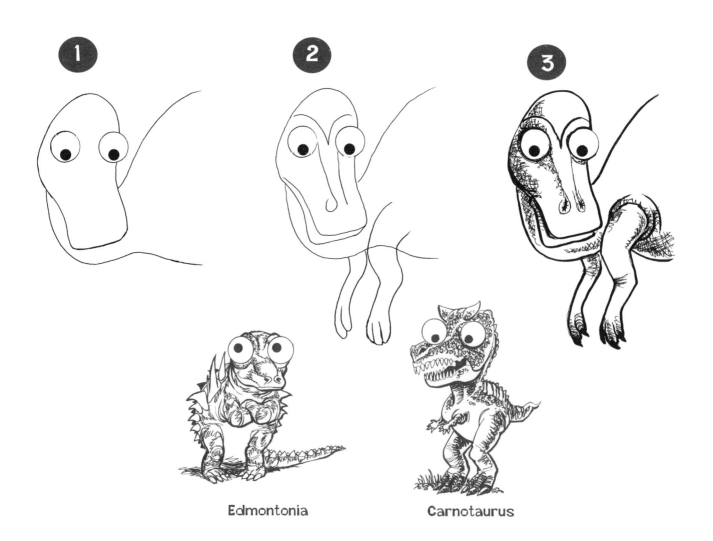

Edmontonia

Carnotaurus

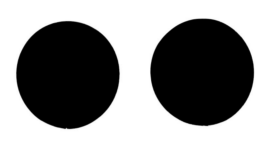

Did you know?

Tyrannosaurus rex was a tough guy with a swishy stride. To balance its massive head as it walked, *T. rex* would have had to swing its tail and rear end from side to side, just like a fashion model.

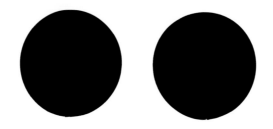

tyrannosaurus rex

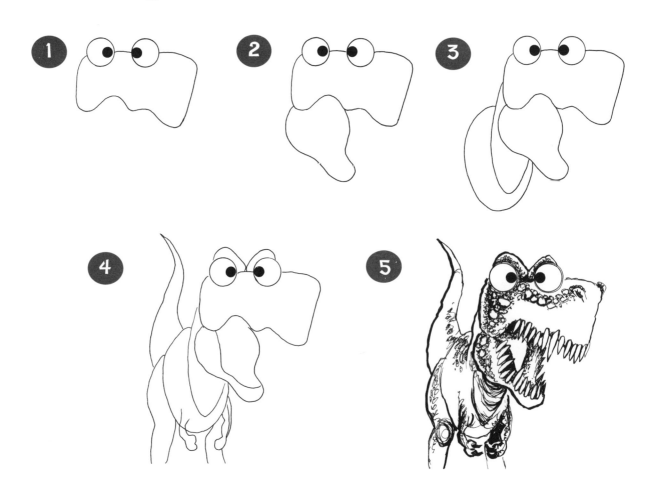

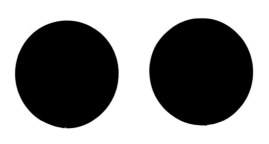

Did you know?

Footprints of dinosaurs are common. However, we do not find the mark of a tail dragging. This tells us that dinosaurs carried their tails in the air.

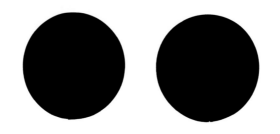

Dunkleosteus

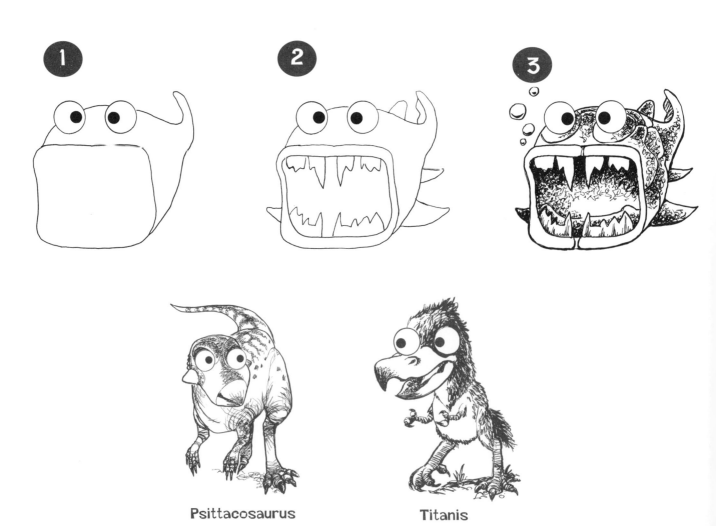

Psittacosaurus   Titanis

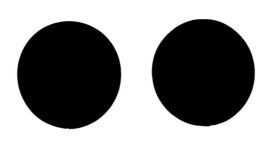

Did you know?

A fossil of *Mei long*, a tiny Chinese dinosaur whose name means "soundly sleeping dragon," was found with its body curled up and its snout tucked under its arm, just like a bird taking a nap. It is one of the smallest known dinosaurs, about the size of a duck.

Hypsilophodon

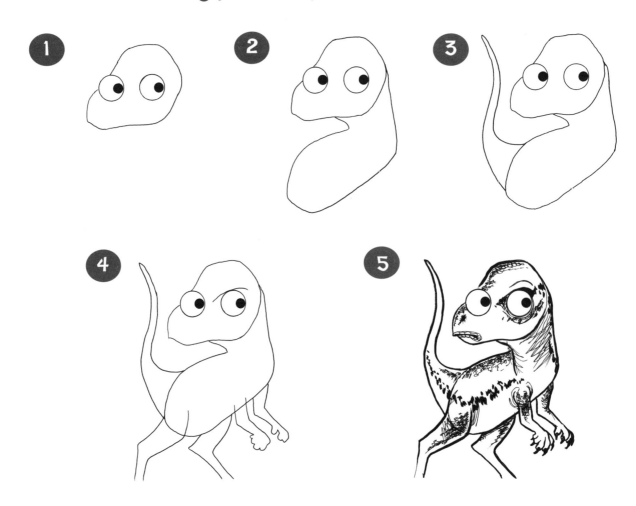

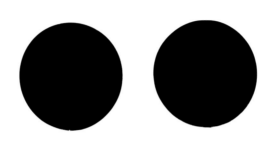

Did you know?

The *Mamenchisaurus* had an elegant look. It had the longest neck of any animal. Its neck was made of 19 vertebrae and was more than 36 feet (11 m) long—over half the length of the whole dinosaur!

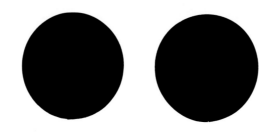

kronosaurus

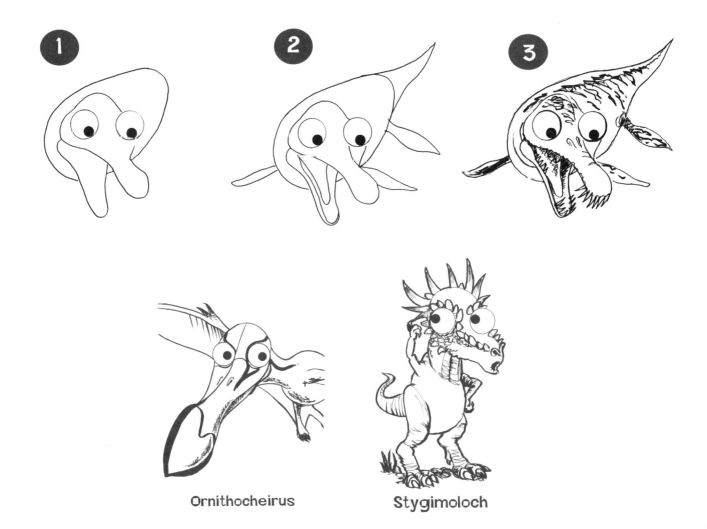

Ornithocheirus   Stygimoloch

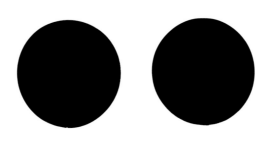

Did you know?

The biggest dinosaurs, the sauropods, laid eggs only the size of a soccer ball. But the babies still had long tails and long necks, so they had to curl up tightly in the eggs.

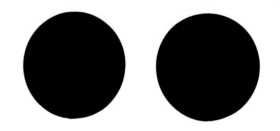

Saltasaurus

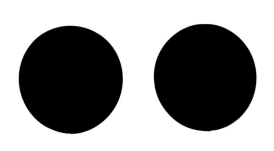

Did you know?

Just like puppies, baby dinosaurs had big heads and big feet.
The fancy horns and head crests were seen only on adults.

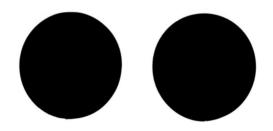

Heterodontosaurus

Coelurosauravus

Koolasuchus

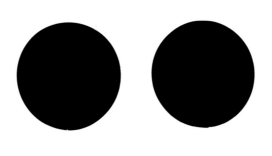

Did you know?

Once in a while fossils show a dinosaur action scene. In one fabulous fossil, a *Velociraptor* looks like it is battling a *Protoceratops*. The *Protoceratops* was biting the arm of the *Velociraptor*, and the *Velociraptor* had its toe claw in the neck of the *Protoceratops*. They died and were buried in place by sand.

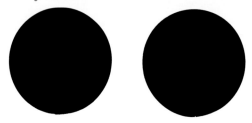

protoceratops

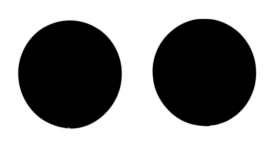

Did you know?

One of the most unusual and mysterious dinosaurs is *Therizinosaurus cheloniformis*. It had claws over 2 feet (61 cm) long on its front limbs! Because the claws were very thin and straight, scientists aren't sure how they were used.

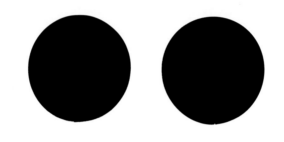

Cetiosaurus

Therizinosaurus

Metriorhynchus

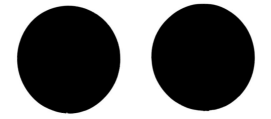

Did you know?

Young dinosaurs had growth spurts just like teenage humans. A teenage *Apatosaurus* could have gained 32 pounds (15 kg) in a day. It did not, however, hog the phone or the bathroom mirror.

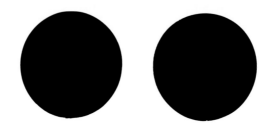

teleosaurus

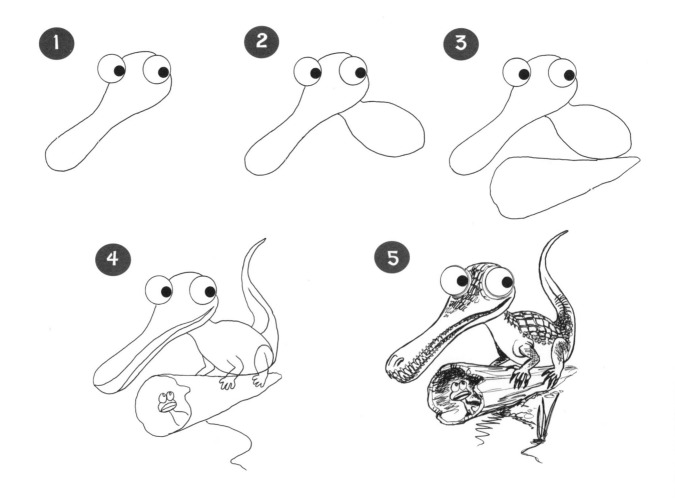

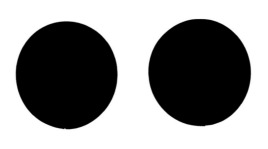

Did you know?

Dinosaurs lived on Earth for 163 million years. If you were to imagine the time from then until now condensed into one year, the dinosaurs lived from about January 1 to September 20. Humans would have just begun living on December 31.

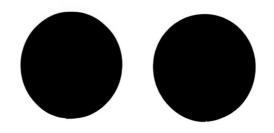

Muttaburrasaurus

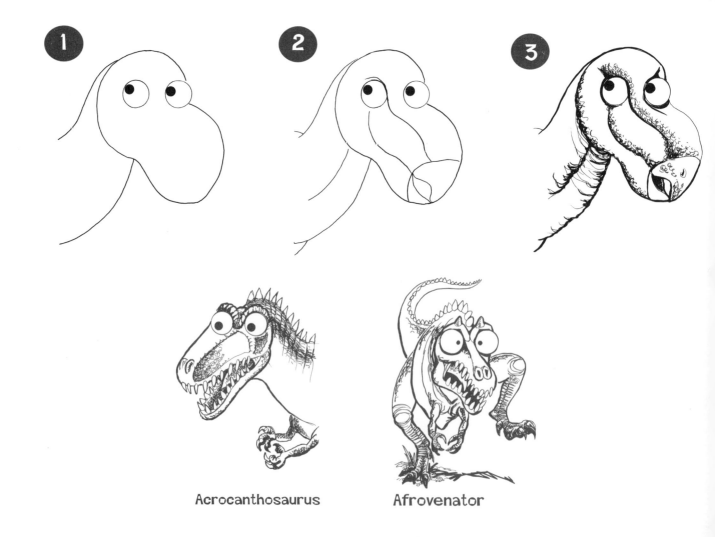

Acrocanthosaurus   Afrovenator

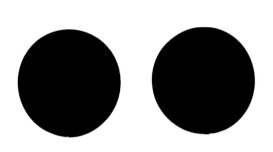

Did you know?

The word "dinosaur" is Latin for "terrible (dino) lizard (saur)." They're not lizards, but the name is too popular to change now!

Staurikosaurus

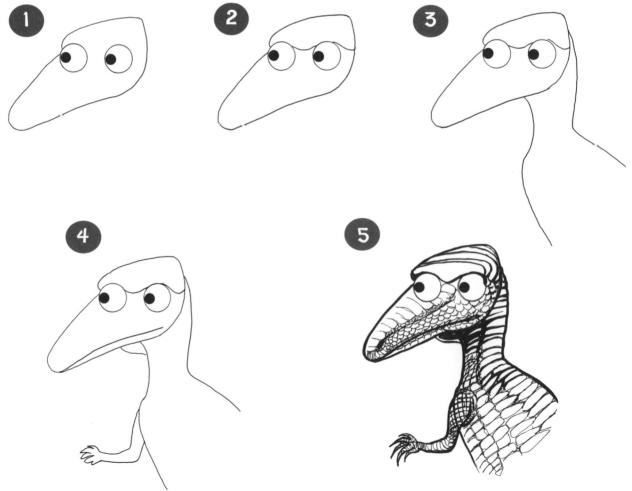

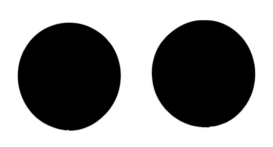

Did you know?

We can't know for sure what color dinosaurs were, but we can guess. Paleontologists think that some may have had "camouflage" markings to blend in with their surroundings. But it is also likely that many dinosaurs were as brightly colored as today's birds and reptiles.

Paralititan

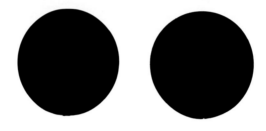

Einiosaurus   Euparkeria

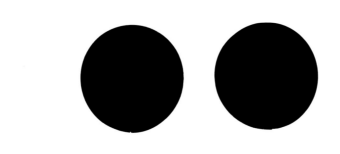

Did you know?

Some fossils have preserved the impression of dinosaurs' skin. Some dinosaurs were covered in bumps like a football, others had pentagonal and hexagonal shapes on their skin, some had tiny scales like a snake, and fossils reveal some species had feathers.

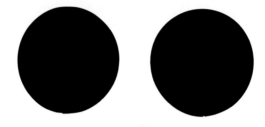

Shantungosaurus

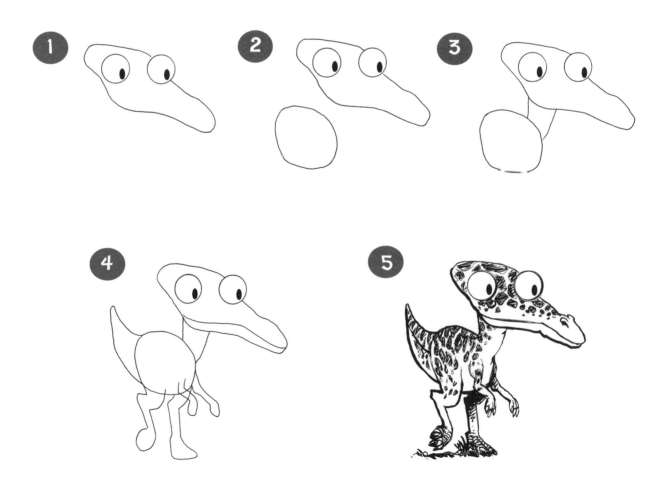

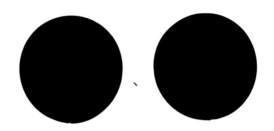

Did you know?

In the late 1800s, sandstone containing half of an unrecognized *Ammosaurus* fossil was sawed into blocks to build a bridge. In 1969, more fossils were recovered when the bridge was demolished.

Xiphactinus

Ceratosaurus

Tuojiangosaurus

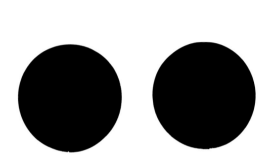

Did you know?

Some dinosaurs didn't have teeth. Instead of chewing, a few dinosaurs swallowed stones, which then ground their food inside their digestive tracts, much like the gizzards of modern birds.

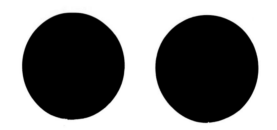

tenontosaurus

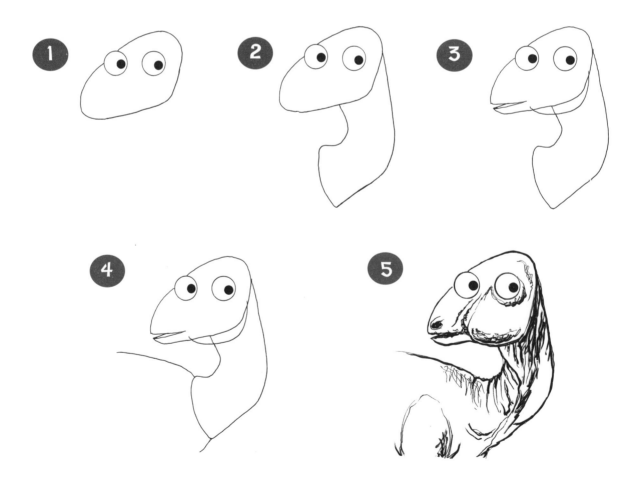

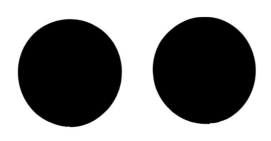

Did you know?

It is very, very hard to tell if a dinosaur fossil was a boy or a girl.
One dinosaur was found, however, that had two unhatched
eggs inside, so we know that one was a girl.

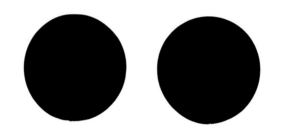

scutellosaurus

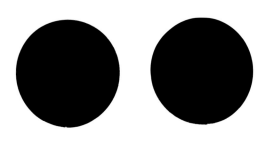

Did you know?

One of the largest pterosaurs was the *Quetzalcoatlus northropi*. Its wings spanned the length of 8 bathtubs (39 ft; 12 m) but it weighed only as much as an average man (180 lb; 82 kg). To be so light, its bones were hollow, much like those of modern birds.

tylosaurus

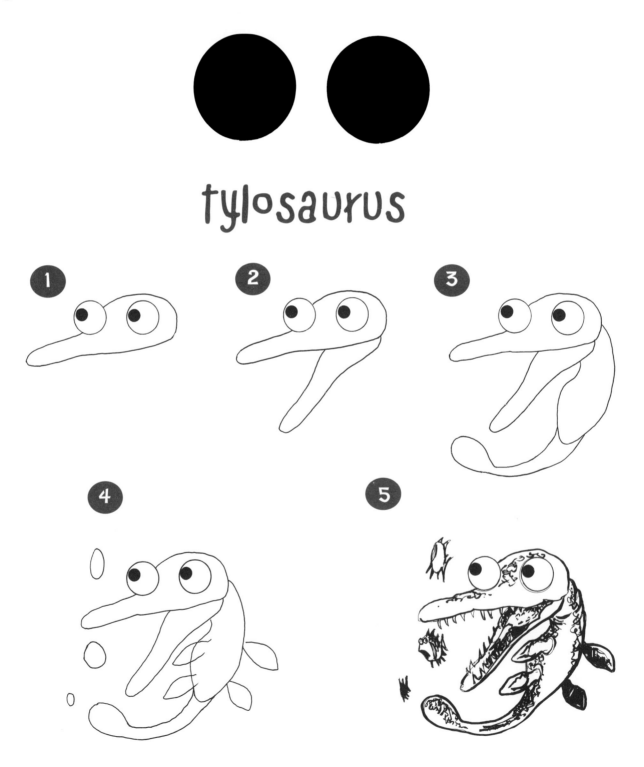

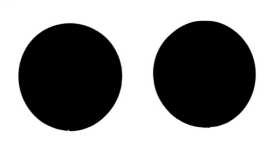

Did you know?

Pachycephalosaurus had a helmet-like skull, which was up to 9 inches (23 cm) thick! By comparison, a human skull is only .25 inches (0.64 cm) thick.

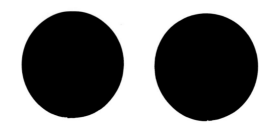

Pachycephalosaurus

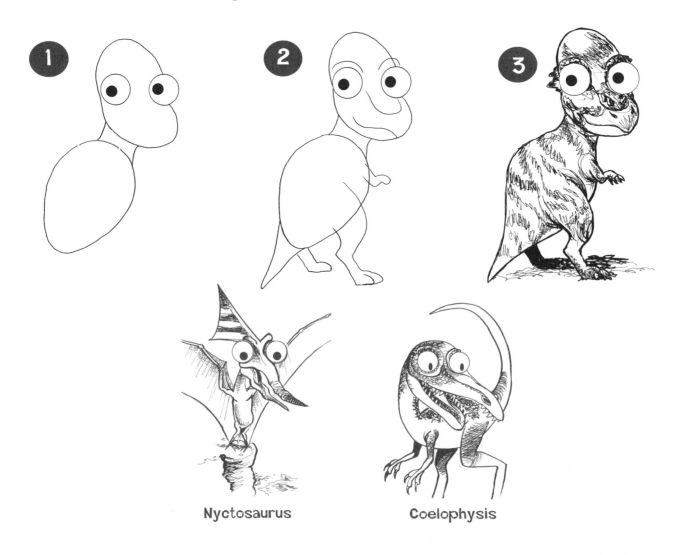

Nyctosaurus

Coelophysis

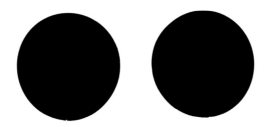

Did you know?

Dinosaur tails could make great defensive weapons. *Diplodocus* could use its super long tail as a whip. *Stegosaurus* had foot-long (30 cm) spikes at the end of its tail to scare off predators like *Allosaurus*. Some ankylosaurs had massive bony clubs at the ends of their tails that they could swing at an attacker.

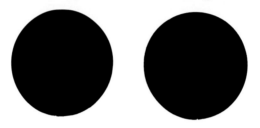

Ouranosaurus

Ankylosaurus   Euoplocephalus

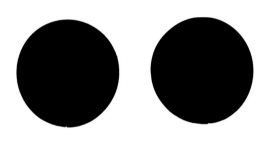

Did you know?

Recent evidence suggests that many dinosaurs traveled together and that some may even have migrated seasonally like birds! Dinosaur fossils have been found above the Arctic Circle, where the food supply could support them only part of the year.

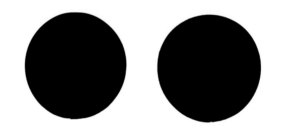

Brachiosaurus

Minmi   Baryonyx

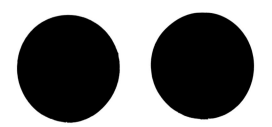

Dimetrodon

try to draw one of these Dinos!

Slimonia

Camptosaurus

Shunosaurus

Megalancosaurus

Diplocaulus

Suchomimus

Mastodonsaurus

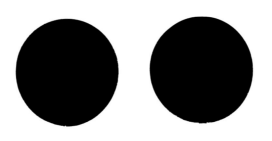

Archaeopteryx

try to draw one of these Dinos!

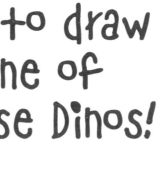

Panderichthys

Plateosaurus

Elasmosaurus

Pteraspis

Hovasaurus

Herrerasaurus

Champsosaurus

Eryops

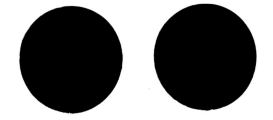

Keep Going!

Don't stop drawing! The more you draw, the better you'll get. The better you get, the more you'll want to draw. Nifty, huh?

Remember, you don't have to be great at drawing to love it!

Imperfection is Perfection ...

and sometimes pretty funny!

Andrews McMeel Publishing, LLC
an Andrews McMeel Universal company
1130 Walnut Street, Kansas City, Missouri 64106

www.andrewsmcmeel.com

15 16 17 18 19 LEO 10 9 8 7 6 5 4 3 2 1

ISBN: 978-1-4494-6806-4

Made by:
Leo Paper/Heshan Astros Printing Ltd.
Address and place of production:
Industrial Development Area, Xijiang River
Gulao Town, Heshan, Guangdong, China
1st printing - 4/6/15

ATTENTION: SCHOOLS AND BUSINESSES

Andrews McMeel books are available at quantity discounts with bulk purchase for educational, business, or sales promotional use. For information, please e-mail the Andrews McMeel Publishing Special Sales Department: specialsales@amuniversal.com.